ALDO E. AZZOPARDI

MALTA

A COLOUR GUIDE

Miller Distributors Limited

Miller House, Tarxien Road, Airport Way, Luqa Malta.
P. O. Box 25 Malta International Airport LQA 05
Telephone: 664488 Facsimile: 676799

Published and printed by

NARNI - TERNI

MALTA

The land and the people

Lying 90 km to the south of Sicily and 290 km to the north of the African mainland, 1830 km to the east of Gibraltar and 1500 km to the west of Alexandria, Malta and its islands might be said to occupy a position in the center of the Mediterranean.

The group is composed of the islands of Malta, Gozo and Comino all of which are inhabited, and the smaller uninhabited islands of Cominotto, Filfla and St. Paul's Islands.

The total area of the archipelago is 320 km^2. The longest distance in Malta in a south-east/north-west axis is about 27 km and the widest distance is 14 km. The corresponding figures for Gozo are 14 km and 7 km. Comino, the smallest of the inhabited islands being 2.6 km^2. The length of the shoreline around Malta is 136 km and that of Gozo being 43 km. The indentations around the coast form bays, sandy beaches and rocky coves and, more importantly, deep natural harbours.

With a population of around 350,000 crowding an area of 320 km^2 the Maltese Islands can claim to be the most densely populated country in Europe.

As a result of intermarriages throughout the ages, Semitic, Latin, Rhodian-Greek and a dash of Anglo-Saxon blood has produced a rich diversity of the Maltese physical "type" and it is only where character is concerned that there is conformity. Perhaps because of his fear of being swallowed up in the crowd, the average Maltese will assert his individuality by adding his personal touch to his car, boat, house or any other of his possessions.

Prehistory

At a point of time around 4,000 BC a group of Late Stone-Age Sicilian farming families left their island home to settle in a small group of islands to the south. They brought over with them their domestic animals, pottery, bags of seeds and flint implements.

They were the first Maltese.

In time these early Maltese increased and prospered and gangs of workers could now be spared from the day to day chores so that they could give all of their time to the building of the temples.

The new immigrants were familiar with the use of copper although the tools they used were still being chipped out of flint as they had been for thousands of years.

At one time it was believed that the temple builders succumbed to an invasion of fresh migrants who exterminated, or enslaved, the original settlers and took over the land. The invasion theory cannot be entirely ruled out and still has its adherents. If there was an invasion, the new arrivals, who, originally, hailed from the heel of Italy would have had no difficulty in overcoming the remnants of the original stock who colonized the islands some 2,200 years before.

If the first settlers were peaceful farmers (no trace of weapons of the period have been discovered) the newcomers were more belligerent. These bronze-age farmers, there is some evidence to show that they were also pastoralists, were less

civilized than the folk they had supplanted, they built no temples but re-used the older, copper-age, temples as cemeteries; their dead were cremated within the walls and the ashes were deposited in the ruins of the once hallowed buildings.

The bronze-age farmers were not allowed to enjoy their islands in peace because after some 600 years of their arrival a new wave of bronze-using warriors invaded the land, and this time it was definitely an invasion, and made it their home. This event took place around 1,200 BC. Imitating their warlike predecessors, they established their settlements in easily defensible positions. The last of the three ages of antiquity — the Iron-Age — is represented in the Maltese Islands by the remains of a single settlement at Bahrija (circa 900 BC).

The Phoenicians

Their homeland a narrow coastal plain, and hemmed in by their enemies between the mountains and the Mediterranean, the only direction in which the Phoenicians could expand was seawards.

The Maltese islands with their fine natural harbours was one such outpost which the Phoenicians founded around 800 BC. As it was in other countries, so it was in Malta: having gained a foothold as traders, they gradually intermarried and integrated with the bronze-age farmers. This assimilation did not, of course, take place overnight, but when it eventually did happen, the new race became the rootstock of the Maltese People, and the language of these people the basis of the Maltese Language.

The larger island was now called M-L-T (Malet: meaning shelter) and the smaller island was named G-L (Gol, after the broad beamed trading vessel).

At this period of the story of Malta we are in the realm of written history, and it is recorded that overlooking the two main harbours in Malta were famous temples dedicated to Phoenician Deities — one in what is now the Grand Harbour, probably under the foundations of Fort St. Angelo, sacred to Melkart and another dedicated to Astarte in the aforementioned Tas-Silg area.

In the case of the Maltese Islands the Phoenicians did venture inland because their remains have been found in several places, even as far as Rabat in the center of the island of Malta.

The weaving industry that flourished before the arrival of the Phoenicians probably received an added boost and a wider export market. Pottery was now thrown on a wheel instead of being coiled as was previously the case.

The links between the Phoenician colonies and the Mother Country were never very strong and when the Phoenician homeland was overrun it was the Phoenician colony of Carthage that took over the rôle of Mother Country.

In many sectors of the Mediterranean littoral the Phoenician/Carthaginians strove to establish a sphere of influence, their chief rivals in this respect being the Greeks. Surprisingly, in the Maltese Islands these differences did not seem to exist: it is not known how many Greeks lived, co-existed rather, with the Phoenicians and the Carthaginians on the Island, but some undoubtedly did — civic institutions resembled their Greek counterparts and Greek coins and pottery have been found on the islands.

The Romans

The three Punic Wars were to last for over a hundred years and during this struggle between the Carthaginians and the Romans, Sicily and its appendage, the Maltese islands, were to occupy central stage in the theatre of war for the control of the Mediterranean.

By the end of the First Punic War, in 241BC, the whole of Sicily had been ceded to the Romans but the Carthaginians were allowed to retain the Maltese Islands.

Peace did not last long, however, because in 218 BC a second war broke out and, learning from their past mistakes, the Romans were determined to capture the islands.

Apparently the invasion did not present great difficulties and it has been suggested that the Phoenicians on the Island turned against their Carthaginian cousins and handed over the garrison to the invading Romans. The Maltese were treated more like allies than as a conquered people which lends some substance to the "collaboration" theory. The Maltese kept their Punic traditions and language and their gods. The two larger islands were renamed Melita and Gaulos and it has been tentatively suggested that the name Melita was not a Romanized version of the Phoenician Malet, but derived from **mel** (honey) for which the islands were then famous.

With Carthage destroyed in the Third Punic War, and the Greeks overcome, the Mediterranean became a Roman Lake — the Mare Nostrum — the areas of conflict of imperial conquest now being the lands bordering this sea.

The Romans built the city of Melita, itself bearing the same name as that of the island, the city was built over an older, Punic settlement in what is now the Rabat/Mdina area in Malta, and also another town in Gozo under what is now Victoria (Rabat).

Saint Paul

The shipwreck of St. Paul in 60AD is recorded in some detail in the Acts of the Apostles, and a Pauline tradition of long standing supported by archeological excavations carried out at San Pawl Milqghi prove beyond doubt that his arrival in Malta is a historical fact and it is also a fact that during his three-month stay on the Island he sowed the first seeds of the Christian Religion to which Maltese people overwhelmingly belong, but inevitably, a number of legends have grown up over the centuries, some verging on the impossible, but others not without a grain of truth.

The Apostle Paul was, at this time, being conducted to Rome under arrest to be judged before Caesar as was his right as a Roman Citizen. Amongst the other prisoners was the physician St. Luke who recorded the account of that eventual journey.

The nearest habitation to the place of shipwreck was the villa of Publius, the Chief Man of the Island, all those who had been shipwrecked spent three days there and after they had regained their strength they moved on to Melita the chief town of the island. In the city Paul cured Publius' father of a fever after which the Chief Man of the Island was converted to Christianity and later ordained Bishop by St. Paul. St. Publius being the first bishop of Malta.

After three months, by which time, the sea was again reckoned to be safe for navigation, and loaded with gifts from his Maltese friends, Saint Paul sailed away to Rome and to his subsequent martyrdom. When the Roman Emperor Constantine embraced Christianity and made it the official religion of the Empire it may be assumed that Christian worship was better organised and that a number of places of assembly were built in various places in the islands. Tradition has it that one such church was built on the site of the palace of Publius, where St. Paul had cured the father of the Chief Man of the Island. Many times rebuilt, the site is now occupied by the Cathedral Church dedicated to Saint Paul at Mdina.

An Empire in Decline

When the Roman Empire had been divided between the two sons of the Emperor Theodosius, Malta and its islands came under the Empire of the East which had its capital in remote Byzantium (modern day Istanbul). Very little is known of Maltese history regarding the four centuries starting from around the year 400AD. This was the period of the break-up of the old Roman Empire, the time when Vandals and Goths carried all before them in Spain and in North Africa and, indeed, on the Italian mainland, the City of Rome itself was taken. The Byzantines, however, were more successful in warding off the attacks of the barbarians largely because of their powerful navy.

About the middle of the 6th Century the lands under Byzantine domination were organised into a series of military provinces or **Themes**.

The Arabs

The Arab attacks on the islands started from around the year 836 during which time Malta and its islands were still under Byzantine rule, but the islands were only overcome in the year 870 by Aglabid Arabs originating from what is now Tunisia who used Sicily as a springboard for their invasion, that island having been occupied by them some thirty years previously.

To better protect their new territories the Moslems sectioned off a part of the old Roman town of Melita and defended it with a ditch, calling this citadel **Mdina**, and did the same thing to the capital of the sister island, Gozo; the élite of the small number of Arabs, then on the islands, probably dwelt in these towns but Arab villages were scattered on both islands; such as **Baħrija** in Malta (baħarija: Arabic for oasis) and the village of **Għarb** in Gozo (għarb: Arabic for West — that hamlet being the most westerly of the Maltese Islands).

The name of the two principal islands, Melita and Gaulos, were changed to Malta and Għawdex and two of the smaller islands were named Kemmuna and Filfla, named after the cummin seed and peppercorn respectively. The Arabs introduced the water-wheel, the **sienja**, an animal-driven device for raising water, now practically obsolete, and, much more importantly, the cultivation of the cotton-plant, the mainstay of the Maltese economy for several centuries.

The Middle Ages

The Arabs in Sicily were divided, and taking advantage of the situation, Count Roger the Norman, after a series of compaigns, subdued that island to Norman Rule.

Count Roger had invaded the islands to make sure his southern flank was secure from a possible Arab attack, having reduced the Arabs to a state of vassalage and releasing the foreign Christian slaves, he returned to Sicily without even bothering to garrison his prize.

In Sicily itself the Normans followed the same enlighted policy and although the Christian Faith was regarded as the official religion there, nobody was persecuted because of his race or for his religious beliefs.

In 1127, Roger II the son of Count Roger, led a second invasion of Malta; having overrun the Island he placed it under a more secure Norman domination under the charge of a Norman governor, he also garrisoned with Norman soldiers the three castles then on the islands. From about this period the Maltese moved back gradually into the European orbit to which they had belonged for a thousand years prior to the Arab interlude.

Because the last Norman king died without a male heir, the new masters of the Maltese islands came, in turn, from the ruling houses of Germany, France and Spain: The Swabians (1194); the Angevins (1268); the Aragonese (1283) and finally, the Castillians (1410).

When the Norman Period came to an end, the Fief of Malta was granted to loyal servants of the Sicilian Crown; these Counts, or Marquises of Malta, as these nobles were styled, looked on the fief simply as an investment — a source for the collection of taxes and something that was bartered or sold when no longer viable.

The last feudal lord of Malta, Don Gonsalvo Monroy, had been expelled from the Island following a revolt and at the Court of Sicily the count demanded that the strongest measures be taken against the insurgents. At the same Court the representatives of the Maltese offered to repay the 30,000 florins originally paid by Monroy for the Fief of Malta; they also ask·d for the Island to be incorporated in the Royal Domains once they had redeemed their homeland. The king, Alphonse V, impressed by their loyalty, called Malta the most **notable** gem in his crown, thus the capital of Malta came to be called Notabile although, then, as now, the Maltese continued to call the town Mdina.

By this time, the Maltese were thoroughly Christianized and the houses of the great Religious Orders were being established in the Island: the Franciscans (1370); the Carmelites (1418); the Augustinians (1450); the Dominicans (1466); and the Minor Observants (1492), while the Benedictine Sisters arrived in 1418.

In 1429 a determined attempt was made by an army of 18,000 Moors from Tunisia under Kaid Ridavan to capture the Maltese islands with the intention of using them as an advance post for further conquests. The Maltese population then numbered between 16,000 to 18,000 with only some 4,000 men under arms. The invaders were beaten back but not before they had captured over 3,000 of the inhabitants as prisoners.

The Knights of the Order of St. John

The visitor arriving by air will probably first notice it in the livery colours of Air Malta, the national airline; he will see it again and again during his stay on the Island: carved on the façade of Baroque palaces, in the form of exquisite filigree brooches, and embossed on many a kitsch, plastic souvenir. It is Eight-pointed, or, as it is better known, the Maltese Cross.

As a military order, the Knights took part in the crusading wars, but when Acre fell in 1291, they were driven off from their last stronghold in the Holy Land.

After a short stay in Cyprus, the Knights, with the assistance of the Genoese, occupied Rhodes. This was to be their home for the next two hundred years.

In Rhodes the Knights perfected the base for their organization that was to make them the most efficient sea-borne warriors of their day.

After wandering for seven years the Knights, and the Rhodian refugees that had attached themselves to them, were offered the Island of Malta for a home by the Holy Roman Emperor, Charles V.

To the relief of the Maltese Nobles, the Knights decided that Mdina, the capital city, was too far inland and they set about establishing themselves in the small village that had grown up behind the old Castel à Mare.

In Birgu the Knights organized themselves along the lines they had evolved during their stay in Rhodes. Their philanthropic origin was not forgotten and amongst the first buildings to be set up was a hospital.

The Order could be described as a multi-national force divided into **Langues** according to the nationality of its members, these langues, or **tongues**, were: Auvergne, Provence, France, Aragon, Castile, England, Germany and Italy. Each langue had its own **Auberge**, or headquarters, as well as a specific duty traditionally assigned to it, each langue was also responsible for the defence of a particular post, such as a section of a bastion or tower.

As if to prove the inadequacy of the defences of the islands, in 1547, and again in 1551, the Turks launched two attacks against the islands, the latter being particularly calamitous. Ravaging the Maltese countryside and ignoring the fortified towns, the Turks then turned their attention to the island of Gozo and carried away the entire population into slavery.

That same year the Turks drove the Knights out of Tripoli. These attacks stung the Knights into feverish activity to improve the islands' defences in anticipation of another, and possibly bigger, attack.

The Great Siege

"Nothing is better known than the siege of Malta" wrote Voltaire two hundred years after the event, and for the Maltese people today the statement still rings true.

The bare bones of the narrative are as follows:

On the 18th May, 1565, the Ottoman Turks and their allies pitted 48,000 of their best troops against the islands with the intention of invading them, and afterwards to make a thrust into Southern Europe by way of Sicily and Italy.

Against them were drawn up some 8,000 men: 540 Knights; 4,000 Maltese; and the rest made up of Spanish and Italian mercenaries.

Landing unopposed, the first objective of the Turks was to secure a safe anchorage for their large invasion fleet, and with that in mind, launched their attack on St. Elmo. After a heroic resistence of thirtyone days the fort succumbed to the massive bombardment and continuous attacks of the Turks. After the fort had been reduced, the Ottomans turned their attention to the two badly fortified towns overlooking the harbour. Subjected to a ceaseless bombardment, and repulsing attack after attack; behind the crumbling walls, the Christian forces, against all odds, kept the enemy at bay until a small relief force of some 8,000 troops arrived from Sicily (a smaller relief force of 600 men had previously landed at about the time that St. Elmo had fallen).

Totally demoralized, as the Turks were, by losses from disease, fire and steel, added to the fact that their supplies were running low, they were in no position to offer an effective resistente, and the Turks retreated never again to attempt another invasion in that part of the Mediterranean.

The Foundation of Valletta

The idea of fortifying the rocky and steep-sided Mount Sciberras had occured to the Knights on their arrival in 1530, but because time was not on their side, they limited themselves to building a fort at its very tip, instead.

If other Grand Masters studied the possibilities of such a project, La Valette was obsessed with the idea; as soon as he had been elected to the Grand Mastership in 1557 he invited foreign military engineers, famous in their time, to prepare the plans, but the Great Siege put a stop to all that.

No sooner was the siege lifted that the plans for the fortress city were again revived, but as a first step the ill-fated Fort St. Elmo was at once rebuilt.

Pope Pius IV sent his military engineer, Francesco Laparelli, and the planning of the new town started in earnest.

When Laparelli departed from the Island he left his Maltese assistant, Gerolamo Cassar, to continue the work he had started. La Valette died in 1568 and was buried in the Church of Our Lady of Victories, the first building to be erected. Other Grand Masters continued to embellish the new city and, in time, all the important buildings of the Order were enclosed within its walls: the Auberges of the Langues of the Order; the Grand Master's Palace with its Armoury; the Co-Cathedral and other churches; the Hospital; the Courts of Justice and the palatial houses of individual Knights, rich Maltese citizens, and ecclesiastics.

The Fall of the Order

When the Order made Malta its home, for the first time the masters of the Maltese lived on the Island itself, and wealth poured **into** the Island, rather than the other way round.

The Knights of the Order of St. John came from the noblest and richest families of Europe and a Knight was expected to pass on his property to the Order on his death, but it was not unusual for a member of the Order to make gifts and endowments during his lifetime as well.

Six years after the Great Siege the Turks were also defeated at sea, in the Battle of Lepanto, in which the galleys of the Order participated.

The finances of the Order were now in a precarious position. Unemployment was rife and poverty was widespread.

Towards the end of the 18th Century matters for the Order were going from bad to worse: in France, where most of her overseas property lay, the possessions of the Order were taken over by the Republican Government and French refugees, fleeing to Malta from the Revolution, were an added drain on the treasury of the Order. In the wake of his victorious Italian campaign, Napoleon confiscated the Order's property in that country as well.

At the time the last Grand Master of Malta, Ferdinand von Hompesch, was being elected, Napoleon was making his plans to take over the Island.

The French

Napoleon's capture of Malta in June 1798 cannot be counted as one of his military triumphs.

The Grand Master capitulated without offering any resistence and Napoleon made his grand entry into Valletta and within a week Von Hompesch, accompanied by a few knights, left the Island unwept, unhonoured, and unsung.

The Maltese felt that they had been led down by the Order, but before they could attempt any resistence they were talked into submission by the Bishop. Maltese that had served in the Order's army and navy were recruited into the French Republican forces, and other regiments were raised for garrison duties on the Island itself.

Nobility was, of course, abolished and all armorial bearings were to be removed.

After stripping the palaces, Auberges and other buildings of everything of value, Napoleon, conveniently forgetting his promises, next turned his attention to the churches; only such articles that were indispensable for the "exercise of the cult" were left while all other valuables were removed and priceless works of art in gold and silver melted down into lingots.

Nominally the Order had held the Island of Malta in fief from the King of Sicily (since 1735 this island had been amalgamated with the State of Naples and was then known as the Kingdom of the Two Sicilies), and it was to the King of the Two Sicilies that the Maltese now turned for aid and protection. At the same time deputies were despatched to seek aid from the allies of the King, the British.

A small number of British troops were landed and the French in Gozo surrendered in October 1798, the Sicilian flag being hoisted on the ramparts.

As the siege wore on, the French penned in the fortifications were prevented from receiving aid because of the British blockade, while the Maltese, by this time, aided by Italian and British troops, did not have the means of assaulting the formidable bastions.

The French, having arrived at the end of their tether, were

ready to capitulate but the troops of Napoleon proudly refused to submit to the Maltese rebels.

The British, on the other hand, anxious to deploy their troops and warships in other theatres of war, were eager to speed up the surrender of the French in Malta.

The Maltese had borne the brunt of the fighting and other privations, but when the capitulation was being drafted and signed neither they, nor their representatives, were allowed to participate in the negotiations.

The National Congress was dissolved and the Maltese Battalions disbanded; a Maltese regiment formed by the British, under British officers was, however, retained.

The British

Once the French were expelled from the Island, the British were not so much interested in keeping Malta, as keeping the French out, in fact, at the Treaty of Amiens (1802), that brought hostilities between Britain and Frrance to an end, it was decided that Malta was to be returned to a reformed Order of St. John under the protection of the Kingdom of the Two Sicilies and that her neutrality was to be guaranteed by all the Great Powers.

The Maltese, in their majority, were thoroughly opposed to such an arrangement. If Britain refused sovreignty over the Island, it was up to the Islanders themselves to decide what was to be their fate.

Italian continued to be the language of culture and learning as it had been for centuries before, and official proclamations were phrased in the Italian tongue.

With the British in command of the sea, all mercantile shipping was obliged to call at the Valletta Harbour for clearance by the British Navy, and before long, the Maltese Islands became the most important centre of trade in the Mediterranean.

Under the Treaty of Paris (1814) the Island was confirmed as a British Possession.

With the cessation of hostilities, Malta lost its favoured position under the protection of the british Navy and as a plague epidemic carried away thousands, an era of wealth and prosperity for the Maltese people came to an end.

As steam replaced sail, Malta became an important coaling station, all the more so after the opening of the Suez Canal in 1869. The dockyards were expanded and provided work for a sizeable section of the population. Agriculture was encouraged to make the Island Fortress as self-sufficient as possible and the growing of potatoes, now a major agricultural export, was introduced. The ever present problem of the water supply also received urgent attention.

Prosperity brought about a rapid rise in the population and emigration was actively encouraged to ease the burden on the Italian political refugees of the **Risorgimento** sought refuge in Malta and the example of these Italian patriots had the effect of further fanning the flames of Maltese Nationalism.

At the insistence of the Maltese a Council of Government was set up in 1835.

The military worth of Malta and its islands was to be demonstrated during the Crimean War (1854-56) when the Island Fortress became a rear base for the departure of troops and a receiving station for casualties.

Imperial policy dictated that Britain take Malta under its wing and anglicize, as far as possible, the local population. An "upstart", educated in an English university, or an English military academy, was looked down upon by an upper-class intellectual brought up and schooled in the Italian language. Before long, the Language Question, as it came to be called, lost its shibboleth value and the fight resolved itself on which of the two languages, English or Italian, were to be taught in Government schools. The Maltese tongue, the language of the people, was to receive a welcome boost from the pro-British faction which promoted the vernacular in favour of Italian as a second language.

In the meantime the question of proper representation was inching slowly towards self-determination.

The First World War placed Malta on a war footing and, as happened in the Crimean War sixty years earlier, Malta was to provide harbour and dockyard facilities to the Allied Navies and her contribution in the cause of sick and wounded soldiers hospitalized on the Island earned Malta the title "Nurse of the Mediterranean".

When peace had been restored hundreds of dockyard, and other workers and servicemen were made redundant and unemployment was widespread.

A National Assembly was set up to make proposals for a new constitution. During one of the public meetings of this Assembly, held on the 7th June 1919, the crowd grew hostile and the troops were called out to restore order. When the troops opened fire on the rioters, three of them were killed while another died of his wounds later. With the new Constitution, that of 1921, Malta was, at last, to be granted Self-Government with responsibility for all internal affairs. The British Government retained control on Defence; Foreign Affairs; and Immigration.

The Path to Independence

For the Maltese People the path to independence was neither smooth nor straight.

By the time Malta was granted Self-Government in 1921 the political factions could be classified into three main groups: the pro-British group that broadly opted for the advancement of the English language and culture, as well as the dissemination of the Maltese language. The pro-Italian group stood for the use of Italian and English but also for the propagation of Italian culture.

A newcomer to the political scene was the Labour Party, then in its infancy, its programme being compulsory education, the promotion of the English and Maltese languages and, as is to be expected, the improvement of working and social conditions.

In the troubles that followed elections were suspended and the Constitution was withdrawn in 1930.

In the following election the pro-Italian party with the support of the Church won at the polls with a great majority. In the political storm that followed the Constitution was again suspended and, one year later, Malta reverted back to colonial rule. The British Government, now in sole control of the Island and unfettered by local political opinion, made Maltese and English the two official languages of the Island, which, in fact, they still are, while the use of Italian was eliminated from administrative circles.

By the time the next constitution was granted World War II had started. When Italy allied herself to Germany Malta was thrown into the front line. The first attack, by Italian bombers, took place on the 11th June 1940. The exodus from the towns into the countryside started soon afterwards.

Using ancient catacombs and a disused railway tunnel as shelters against air-raids, other tunnels were excavated in the living rock for the same purpose. War in the Mediterranean theatre was predictable, yet when it did come the Island was poorly equipped to defend itself: the only fighter planes were four antiquated Gloster Gladiators. These planes were augmented with a few Hurricanes some weeks later. Against these, the Italian **Regia Aeronautica** could count on two hundred aircraft stationed in Sicily, a mere hundred kilometres from Malta. The Axis (the Germans and the Italians) were clearly anxious to occupy Malta to make sure that their supply line between Sicily and North Africa was not cut and when the Germans moved the **Luftwaffe** into Sicily the bombing was intensified.

As a result many buildings, especially those in the harbour area and near the airfields were flattened or badly damaged. In June 1941 Hitler attacked Russia and the **Luftwaffe** in Sicily diverted most of its planes to that front. The air-raids on Malta eased, but did not cease entirely; at the same time, having received reinforcements, Malta took to the offensive and submarines and aircraft based on the Island attacked Axis shipping as well as ground targets in Sardinia, Sicily and even Tripoli; furthermore, by intercepting supplies from Sicily to North Africa, Rommel was deprived of many essential supplies. On 26th July 1941 the only seaborne attack, that directed against the Grand Harbour by Italian E-boats, was brave and dashing, was unsuccessful. It was radar that had alerted the Maltese gunners and foiled the E-boat attack.

When the **Luftwaffe** was again in Sicily in full complement the bombing commenced once more and Malta was, once again, thrown on the defensive. Munition, fuel and other stores were running low and food was in short supply.

Throughout this ordeal, despite continuous air-raids, lack of practically all necessities, and an acute food shortage, the Maltese soldiered on. A third of the anti-craft crews were Maltese and they soon made a name for themselves for their bravery and efficiency.

On the 15th of April 1942 King George VI awarded the George Cross Medal to "... the brave people of the Island Fortress of Malta".

If the morale of Malta's defenders was high, the material resources of the Island were low; with supply ships being intercepted and destroyed by Axis aircraft and submarines the situation was desperate, by July 1942 the supply of vital provisions was calculated to last two weeks. Although badly mauled, the "Santa Maria Convoy" limped into the Grand Harbour on the 15th August of that year and the situation was saved.

With replenished stores and the arrival of some hundred Spitfires, the tables, at last, were being turned.

Although Malta was still under attack, by June 1943, it was considered sufficiently safe for King George to visit the Island to a huge welcome by the Maltese people whom he had so singularly honoured.

A month later, using Malta as an advance base, the Allies invaded Sicily and the war moved away from the Island.

True to their promise made during the War, the British restored Self-Government.

Fresh elections were held and the pro-Italian exiles were repatriated. With most of the inhabitants being homeless, reconstruction was the first priority of the newly elected Labour Government but social conditions were also improved.

In the dockyard area, especially, the trade union movement grew in strength as workers everywhere were becoming conscious of their rights.

Three years later, following a split in the Labour Party, the Nationalist Party headed a Coalition Government, this party now strove to obtain a Dominion Status for the Island. The Nationalists were formerly the pro-Italian party but, since the post-war years, the image of this party was to change gradually and in the end they were even accused of being pro-British! Originally being the party of the intelligentsia, the party now attracted numerous workers within its ranks.

On the return of the Labour Party to office, a request for integration was made to the British Government with Maltese representation at Westminster. When the British cooled to the idea after evincing an initial interest the Labour Party went to the other extreme and insisted on Independence, and the Church was accused of having undermined the Integration plan by insisting that its ancient privileges be safeguarded; the acrimonies that followed were to cost the Labour Party many votes.

The Constitutional Party, the original pro-British party, died a natural death, its mission having been accomplished.

In the wake of fresh elections and confirmed by a referendum, Malta achieved Independence within the Commonwealth on 21st September 1964 with the Queen of England as the nominal Queen of Malta.

Under the next Labour Government, Malta was declared a Republic with Sir Anthony Mamo as its first President.

On the 31st March 1979, at the termination of the Military Base Agreement, the last British serviceman left the Island and Malta entered into its self-imposed state of neutrality.

The tourism was promoted and foreign investors were encouraged to set up factories in Malta.

In the latest elections, those of 1987, the Nationalists were returned to power and, although they adhere strictly to the concept of neutrality, they made it their declared policy of applying for membership in the European Economic Community — if the conditions are right — and, with that in view, the present Government is conforming to European standards as much as possible in anticipation of forming part of the Community.

The Maltese are a proud and independent people but in their heart of hearts they realise that financially Malta cannot stand alone. The Labour Party desired integration with Britain, and the old-time Nationalists had yearned for integration with Italy. By joining the European Economic Community it is possible that the Maltese people will achieve their aspirations without having to sacrifice their sovereignty in the process.

A view of the
Fort St.
Michael at
Senglea Point
in the
foreground.

Valletta

When Grand Master Jean Parisot de la Valette laid the foundation stone of **Humilissima Civitas Vallettae** the last thing that he had in mind was a city of fine palaces, Valletta was intended as a fortress to protect the two harbours on either side of the rocky peninsula on which it was to be built.

The first buildings to be erected were the Auberges, these were the headquarters of the different ethnic groups into which the Knights were divided.

The National Library, the **Biblioteca**, was the last building to have been built by the Order having been finished in 1796. It houses a rich collection of books as well as medieval manuscripts and the archives of the Order. As a memento one can buy a photocopy of the deed of Emperor Charles V in which he granted Malta and its islands in fief to the Order in 1530.

Even if the Opera House has yet to rise from the ashes of the Blitz (some are of the opinion that a multi-storey car park should be built there instead), music lovers and balletomanes can still go to Manoel Theatre. This gem of a building was built in 1732 and has recently been restored to its former glory for, as its builder Grand Master Anton Manoel de Vilhena would have said it, "... the honest recreation of the people". For art lovers there are the Museum of Fine Arts and the Cathedral Museum.

Valletta boasts of three Parish Churches and a host of others, but pride of place must go to St. John's Co-Cathedral.

The plain exterior of this edifice grossly belies its sumptuous interior: no space is left unadorned, the walls are carved and gilt and the painted vaulted ceiling is the masterpiece of Mattia Preti while fourhundred slabs of inlaid marble pave the church, these slabs are emblazoned with the armorial bearings of the more important members of the Order.

In years gone by, people, young people especially, used to troop into Valletta every evening; they filled the many cinemas there, crowded the coffee shops or just strolled up and down the main streets to admire and be admired, followed by a last-minute rush to catch the last bus to the village.

The Triton fountain.   Aerial view of Valletta.

Auberge of Castille

The Auberge of Castille, Leon and Portugal, is the largest and perhaps finest of all the Auberges. Its head was the Grand Chancellor of the Order of St. John.

It was first built in 1574 by Girolamo Cassar on a site originally earmarked for the Magisterial Palace. Extensive reconstructions were undertaken in 1744 during Grand Master Pinto de Fonseca's term of office. Domenico Cachia, the architect responsible for these modifications was influenced by the Prefettura at Lecce and produced a very imposing façade.

Below, the St. Paul's Anglican Cathedral and church of Our Lady of Mount Carmel.

Among the vorious monuments housed in the Upper Barracca gardens, it is interesting to observe the bronze work "Les Gavroches" of the Maltese sculptor Antonio Sciortino (bottom at right).

St. John's Co-Cathedral

In 1573 Grand Master Jean de la Cassière authorized the construction of a conventual church of the Order of St. John. It was completed in 1578 by the Maltese architect Girolamo Cassar. Alessandro Algardi's bas relief of the Saviour surmounting the façade was relocated here in 1850's from its original place in a chapel close to the entrance of the Grand Harbour. The spires on the bell towers were destroyed during the Second World War.

The rectangular Baroque interior was embellished by successive Grandmasters and further enriched by the "Gioja" or present, which every Knight was bound by statute to give on admission to the Order.

Between 1662-67, Mattia Preti "Il Calabrese" painted the life of St. John the Baptist, patron saint of the Order, directly on to the primed stone of the ceiling. The Cottoner brothers paid for this work.

In the ornate Oratory is a 3 by 5 metre painting by Caravaggio depicting the beheading of St. John. This painting is regarded as the master piece of Caravaggio and is the only one of his paintings which bears his signature.

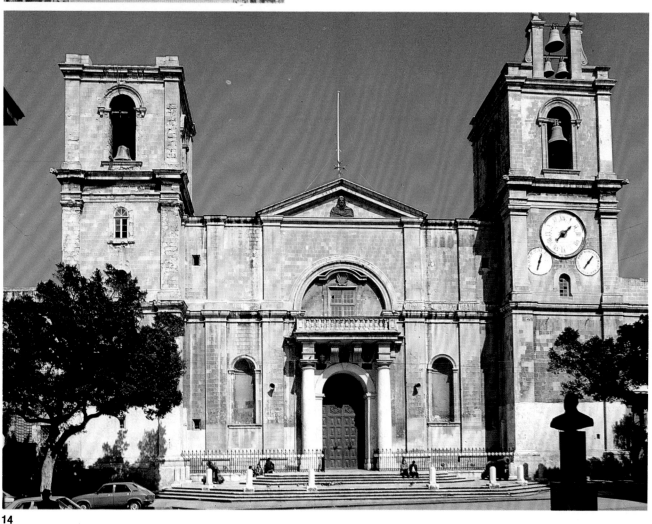

National Museum of Fine Arts

South Street is one of the most elegant streets in the city. It was originally known as Strada del Palazzo after the Magisterial Palace which was to be built here. This street was also known as Strada d'Albergo di Francia after the Auberge de France, destroyed during the last war, situated in it.

The National Museum of Fine Arts is one of the palaces gracing this street. This was among the first buildings erected in Valletta but it was rebuilt in its present form between 1761 and 1765. On the right, white marble bust by the Maltese sculptor Antonio Sciortino.

Auberge de Provence

The Auberge de Provence was built between 1571-75 to a design of the Maltese architect Girolamo Cassar. The façade was re-designed during the first half of the 18th Century. The Auberge was the residence of the Langue de Provence, its Head, the "Grand Commandeur" being the Treasurer of the Order.

From 1824 to 1954 the building housed the British officers' Union Club, and is now the National Museum of Archeology. Below: the sleeping Lady.

The Grand Masters' Palace

Valletta is a city of palaces but for the Maltese, the Grand Masters' Palace is known simply as il-Palazz, **the** Palace.

In its finished form the Palace is built on two floors and occupies an entire block. The two main portals, Baroque and imposing, stand in direct contrast to the unadorned treatment of the rest of the façade; three other side entrances give on to as many streets.

Three of the doorways lead to a spacious courtyard while another portal and a gate lead to a smaller courtyard which is on a slightly higher level. The larger of the two courtyards is known as Neptune's Courtyard from a bronze statue of that god. The smaller courtyard — Prince Alfred's Courtyard is named after one of Queen Victoria's sons to commemorate his visit to Malta in 1858, but this courtyard is better known as that of Pinto's Clock. This clock has four dials showing, besides the time: the day, the month and the phases of the moon. The hours are struck by bronze effigies of Moorish slaves wielding sledge-hammers. It is said to be the work of the Maltese clockmaker Gaetano Vella and built in 1745.

As in Renaissance palaces in Italy, the important storey was the **Piano Nobile**, the first floor; the ground floor being used as stables, service quarters and stores.

The Main Staircase leading up to the **Piano Nobile** was built by Grand Master Hughes de Loubenx Verdala as

The main entrance to the upper floor with the coat-of-arms of the Malta Republic in the foreground.

advertised by the wolf in his coat of arms. The top of the staircase gives on to a lobby formed by the angle where two fo the palace corridors meet.

The right-hand passage leads to what used to be the Palace Armoury but that part of the building is now the seat of the House of Representatives (the Parliamentary Assembly is composed of only one chamber, there is no Upper House).

The lunettes over the windows in this passage are the work of Nicolò Nasoni da Siena and have been painted in the first quarter of the 18th Century. Their opposite numbers have been painted by the Maltese artist Giovanni Bonello some hundred and sixty years later; the whole set, however, is complementary and shows Maltese and Gozitan landscapes as they appeared at those times.

A notable hall in the Armoury Corridor is the Council, or Tapestry, Chamber, which was the place where the members of the Order seat in Council. This chamber was also the seat of the Malta Parliament from 1921 until 1974, before the House moved to its present situation.

On being elected to that high office, a Grand Master was expected to make a gift to the Order — the **Gioja**.

Part of the **Gioja** of Grand Master Ramon Perellos y Rocaful is the priceless set of Gobelins Tapestries that give the name to this chamber. Perellos was elected in 1697 but it was only in 1710 that these tapestries were completed and hung in the place for which they had been created. **Les Tentures des Indes** (the Indian Tapestries) is a vague title for a magnificent rendering of fauna and flora from three continents, the Noble Savage being also very much in evidence.

To the left-hand of the lobby at the top of the Main Staircase is another corridor, known as the Entrance Corridor, this too, like the Armoury Corridor is decorated by paintings of Nicolò Nasini, but this time the subject chosen for the decoration of the lunettes are scenes of naval battles between the Order's galleys and those of the Ottoman Turks, apparently a subject dear to the hearts of these seafaring Knights.

The first door to the right of the lobby leads into the State Dining Room, here the British connection is well represented by several Royal portraits. The next door down the Entrance Corridor leads to the Hall of the Supreme Council, also known as the Throne Room. Like all the other ceilings of the **Piano Nobile**, the wooden ceiling of this hall is elaborately coffered and painted, but the item of greater interest in this hall is a frieze of twelve frescoes by Matteo Perez d'Aleccio who worked in Malta between 1576 and 1581.

Against the far end of the wall is the throne, occupied in turn, by the Grand Masters and the British Governors. Above the throne are now the arms of the Republic of Malta.

Across the hall and opposite the throne a carved minstrels' gallery is let into the wall; this carved and painted gallery is said to have been part of the Order's flagship, the Great Carrack of Rhodes, which was one of the vessels that carried the Knights to Malta.

A door from the Throne Room leads to the Ambassadors' Room, also known as the Red Room from the colour of its damask hanging.

In one of the panels, Knights of the Order are shown holding shields bearing the white eight-pointed (or Maltese) cross on a **red** background; this could be poetic licence on the part of the painter because the battle standard of the Order was a plain white cross on a red background, something like the Danish Flag. A door from the Ambassadors' Room leads to the **Paggeria**, the Pages' waiting room, also known as the Yellow Room from the gold damask covering of its walls.

A door from the Pages' Waiting Room leads into a corridor which is at a right angle to the Entrance Corridor. This corridor is known as the Prince of Wales Corridor in commemoration of a visit by King Edward VII, then Prince of Wales, in 1862.

The rooms giving on to this passage were formerly the private apartment of the Grand Master, afterwards they were used as the offices of the British Governors. These rooms are now the offices of the President of the Republic.

The private chapel of the Grand Master was turned into an office for the use of the Governor's Secretary and the minstrels' gallery that was in it, removed to the Throne Room where it still is. The paintings in this chapel are probably the earliest found in the palace and show episodes from the life of St. John the Baptist, the patron saint of the Order that bears its name.

The Knights frowned upon the use of firearms as being unchivalrous but they were obliged to move with the times.

The collection, as presently displayed, is small but interesting; in the old Armoury, and even more so in engravings of the Armoury as it was at one time, one is impressed by the great number of exhibits, but on the other hand, many of the specimen were repetitous, to the serious student a specimen collection is more interesting.

At the time of the arrival of the Order in Malta, in 1530, the use of firearms was well on the way of revolutionizing warfare — the Great Siege was fought largely with artillery and arquebus but armour still had its uses — a century later breastplates and shields were still being tested against firearms — in the Armoury there are several examples with dents in them to prove that they were proof against ball, in other words "bulletproof".

The Minstrels' Gallery in the Throne Room showing biblical scenes of the "Creation".

Sliema and St. Julians

Around the 1850's Sliema became a summer resort for the well-to-do and, before long, the resort grew into a town. The rich built their villas on the ridge, away from the slummy end where the fisher folk lived. As the British servicement left, the tourists moved in, and the houses of Sliema: the villas and the hovels, were pulled down and block of flats and hotels rose up in their stead. A fort built by the British in 1872 is now an excellent **pizzeria**.

The promenade is probably the most densely populated area in the Island as strollers enjoy the sea-breezes in the cool of the summer evenings. St. Julians, its suburb, can claim an older ancestry. Originally this hamlet sprung up around the old chapel dedicated to Saint Julian, patron of the chase (first built in 1580, but many times rebuilt). The hunting lodges of the Knights have all disappeared except for that of Bali' Spinola who gave his name to the environs of the fishing harbour of St. Julians. Where the old hunting lodges once were are now the large number of hotels, restaurants and pubs that make of St. Julians the most bustling and popular tourist resort in Malta especially with the younger set.

The small balconies on houses along
the waterfront.

The pleasant Karrozzin

The bay of Balluta along the St. Julian waterfront and on the next page, the typical and very colourful boats of the Maltese fishermen anchored in the small port of Spinola.

View of the small
port of Spinola in
the bay of St.
Julian.

On the next
page: a sight
of Vittoriosa

The Three Cities

Collectively known as the Three Cities, individually, the towns by the harbour are known by several names; however, Birgu, Bormla and Senglea are the names by which they are most commonly known.

In the beginning there was Birgu, then a small fishing village sheltering behind a castle of unknown antiquity that stood at the very tip of the peninsula. The castle, as the Castrum Maris, or Castell 'a Mare, is mentioned in several medieval documents. Apparently the Castellan had a measure of autonomy and was independent of the **Università**, the municipal council with its seat at Mdina, and it also appears that the people whose houses were outside the wall of this castle considered themselves as being under the jurisdiction of the Castellan and beyond that of the **Università** which led to much bad blood between the two bodies.

On their arrival in 1530 the Knights decided to settle in Birgu as Mdina was too far inland, and immediately set about protecting that hamlet with bastions. Castell 'a Mare was strengthened and separated from Birgu by a ditch. Not long afterwards, the adjacent peninsula, then uninhabited and known as l'Isla was likewise protected bu bastions and by the time Claude de la Sengle was Grand Master it was sufficiently inhabited to merit the name of "Città Senglea" named, of course, after the Grand Master.

During the Great Siege of 1565 the inhabitants of Birgu and Senglea showed such outstanding courage that the two towns received the honorific titles of Città Vittoriosa (the Victorious City), and Città Invitta (the Unconquered City) respectively.

The conurbation that linked Birgu and Senglea was named "Bormla" and as successive Grand Masters enclosed all three cities with imposing lines of bastions, Bormla received the title of Città Cospicua (the Noteworthy). As Valletta was being built, the Knights transferred their seat of government from Birgu to that town but the three cities were still very much the centre of the naval activities of the Order; here were the shipyards and the arsenals, and here lived the Maltese seamen and ship chandlers.

Piracy was a profession of long standing, but with the arrival of the Order, Maltese corsairs achieved respectability by operating under licence from the Grand Master; and by being taxed on their booty!

Above: a sight of Senglea
Below: the ancient Hospital of Bighi

Tarxien Temples

In no other site in Malta is the evolution of prehistoric temple building better exemplified than it is at the megalithic temples of Tarxien. The earliest temple, now unfortunately in a vestigial state, goes back to around 2,800BC while the more recent of the four temples burst out in a blaze of splendour some seven hundred years later. The spiral, as a decorative motif, is found in many places in Europe from the North Atlantic seaboard to the Aegean; the ones at Tarxien, however, might have been invented, or at least developed, independently. Inside these temples has been found what, for that age, was the most colossal stone sculpture then in existence: originally 2.50 metres in height, the statue, presumably representing a Mother Goddess, has been broken in half and the top part is missing. There is a lot of conjecture about the significance of the Fat Lady statues found in most of the Maltese temples, it is possible that they are examples of female fertility deities prevalent throughout the lands bordering the Mediterranean.

Around 1,800BC the temples, having been abandoned for about two hundred years, were reused by Bronze Age folk as crematoria and as repositories of the ashes of their dead.

On the side, the second Temple with an ancient votive brazier in the centre.
On the following page: a detail of the second temple with a receptacle from the megalithic period; below, the colossal "stone idol", part of a statue that must have measured 2.50 metres in height.

Żabbar Church

The building of the Church of Our Lady of Graces was started in 1641 at the instigation of the Parish Priest Don Francesco Piscopo and was completed in 1660 according to one version, and in 1696 according to another.

A Maltese proverb says "a church is never finished", which is another way of stating that the people in a particular parish are never satisfied with their own church and, depending on their means, are forever improving it, the moving spirit being the ambition that the church in one's village be better and bigger than the church in the next parish. The good people of Żabbar are no exception.

Largely from the private funds of the Parish Priest Andrea Buhagiar, in addition to money collected from the people of Żabbar, work on embellishing the church was started in 1738.

The Maltese architect Giovanni Bonavia redesigned the façade and two belltowers were erected, in addition the church was paved in marble and provided with a crypt.

The main painting of the Madonna and Child is an opera of the painter Alessio Erardi (1669-1727).

Marsaxlokk

Marsaxlokk, the harbour to the south-east, is now a small but picturesque harbour where the brightly coloured fishing boats ride at anchor and where the wives of the fishermen knot nylon string bags for the tourists.

But Marsaxlokk is also a microcosm of the historical past of the Island. A short distance from this village is the archeological site of **tas-Silg**, still in the process of being excavated; at this place are the remains of Late Neolithic megalithic buildings much disturbed by superimposed Punic and Byzantine structures; here too are the only remains of a mosque to be found on the Island. Norman coins have also found at **tas-Silg**.

To oppose the landing of corsairs in that harbour a fort was erected at its entrance by the Order, that of San Lucian; used as a munition depot during World War II, it now houses the Marine Research Centre. Marsaxlokk Bay, of which the fishing harbour of Marsaxlokk forms part, is now being converted into a port for container ships.

Għar Dalam

At the time the Maltese islands were an extension of the Italian mainland, animals like the elephant, hippos, deer and foxes roamed the land. With the rising of the sea-level, or the sinking of the land, or both, the islands were separated from the land mass and these animals were marooned. This took place in the Quaternary Era, some 10,000 years ago, and not during the Pliocene, eleven million to one million years ago, as was once thought to have been the case.

In time these stranded animals gradually evolved into an island sub-race resulting in a degeneration in some of the species.

Fossil bones of animals have been discovered in caves and fissures in various parts of the island, but the largest concentration to be discovered so far is that at Għar Dalam.

In 1917 two human molars were found in this cave and believed, at the time of their discovery, to be those of Neanderthal Man. However, these molars have now been assigned to a much later period and it can be assumed that when the animals died, and their bones carried into Għar Dalam by the action of flowing water, Man had not yet arrived in Malta. Stone Age Man did use Għar Dalam as his abode around 4,000BC but, by this time these animals had become extinct in the Maltese Islands.

Wied iż - Żurrieq and the Blue Grotto

Looking like a miniature fjord, this narrow arm of the sea is an anchorage for boats in calm weather; at the first sign of a storm the boats are winched up a steep slipway and landed.

The boats at Wied iż-Żurrieq were, and still are, used for fishing; now, however, the fishermen are finding out that it is more lucrative to take visitors to the nearby Blue Grotto.

The Blue Grotto.

Ḣaġar Qim

This Copper Age temple was originally built about 2,700 BC but during the same period it underwent several modifications. For some unknown reason the axis of the first temple was altered and the temple itself was several times extended.

The kind of stone used in the building of this temple (Globigerina Limestone) is rather solf and relatively simple to work; possibly for this reason there are several "porthole" openings in Ḣaġar Qim. A monolith on the outside of the temple wall has been tentatively interpreted as evidence of phallic worship.

A pillar "altar" with an unusual palm frond decorative carving has been found in this temple, but not in any other; it is possible that this pillar was not originally part of the temple furniture and it has been placed there at a later date.

Mnajdra

Perhaps having learned that Globigerina Limestone does not resist weathers the builders of Mnajdra constructed this temple out of the harder Coralline Limestone which, however, was difficult to work, while the interior walls were faced with a softer kind of limestone.

The best preserved of the three Mnajdra temples is interesting for the secret chambers that are hidden inside the thickness of its walls; these chambers communicate with the temple proper by holes bored through the wall; it is surmised that statues of gods, or goddesses, could have been placed in front of these holes and the "priest" hiding in the oracle chamber was the voice of the deity as this "spoke" to the faithful. A healing cult could have been practiced in this temple because a number of baked-clay models of parts of the human body, showing symptoms of disease, have been found here.

Ta' Qali Crafts Village

The military airstrip had been abandoned for many years when somebody started using the disused hangar as a workshop for glass-blowing. And so it came about that the Ta' Qali Crafts Village was born.

In a short time the Nissen huts there were taken over by other craftsmen and new huts built. Traditional arts like pottery, silver and gold filigree, and lace making were collected in one place soon to be joined by other, possibly, less traditional, handicrafts.

Among the light industries carried on at Ta' Qali is the making of polished stone ornaments using Malta "marble" as raw material; the Malta Stone workshop carries a sign offering the visitor to take back home a "piece of Malta".

For those who want to take back a piece of Maltese history one can buy a replica of a knight's armour (they come in all sizes) or even a pottery copy of the Fat Lady.

Mosta

Mosta is roughly in the geographical center of the Island of Malta and, in times gone by, it was considered to be far enough inland to be relatively safe from corsair attacks.

The chief attraction is now the monumental church which design was inspired by the Pantheon in Rome. Its dome is the fourth largest in Europe: the three other domes being in Rome, London, and Xewkija in Gozo. The building was started in 1833 and the church was consecrated in 1871; it was built around and over an older church which continued to be used during the time work was in progress. In the machine age in which we are living this sounds like an exceedingly long time, but one should bear in mind that the labour on this church was done on a voluntary basis, in the little spare time the people had at their disposal. This church, like many other of the older churches in Malta, could be said to be a monument of faith. In 1942 a thousand pound bomb penetrated the dome but failed to explode.

Is shown the bomb which hitted the cupola during the last world war without exploding. View of the large interior of Mosta church.

42

Buġibba

Until a few short years ago Buġibba and its extension Qawra were a rocky and barren headland yet not without its points of interest; at its tip is a small coastal battery of the Order which surrounds an older watchtower. Further inland is a small prehistoric temple, in a poor state of preservation, this temple is unique in that it was decorated with carvings of fish (these bas-reliefs are now preserved in the National Museum of Archeology in Valletta). Buġibba and Qawra are now one of the most popular summer resorts to the north of the Island.

St. Paul's Bay

St. Paul's Bay is one of the older seaside resorts. At the turn of the century it was the fashion for persons of means to have a second home on the coast in which to pass the hot summer months in peace and quiet but also in comfort. St. Paul's is now a residential area but an aura of tranquility still pervades the place.

The town of **San Pawl il -Baħar** (more accurately translated as St. Paul by-the sea, rather than St. Paul's Bay) has many reminders of its namesake — the Apostle of the Gentiles. Here one can see **Għajn Rażul**, the Apostle's Fount, at which the saint is reputed to have quenched his thirst following his shipwreck; the church at **tal-Ħuġġieġa**, the church of the bonfire, marking the site where the apostle shook off the viper into the flames; and the church at **San Pawl Milqgħi**, the place where St. Paul was made welcome by Publius, the Roman Governor. A number of churches have been built in succession on this last site and, significantly, in the lowest level of the dig, Roman remains have come to light.

Mellieħa

In the old maps, two landmarks are indicated to the north of the Maltese Islands: the saltpans, and the old church of Mellieħa. The production of salt has been moved to another place (the old saltpans were once sited where the Għadira Bird Sanctuary now stands), but the old semi-underground church dedicated to Our Lady still stands; in it a fresco of the Virgin Mary has, according to tradition, been painted by St. Luke himself who, with St. Paul, was shipwrecked not far from here in the year 60. Scientific study of the icon has assigned it to a more recent, but still very ancient period.

The old saltpans are gone but they have given their name to the town of Mellieħa, **melħ** being the Maltese word for "salt".

Most of the sandy beaches, none of them very big, are found to the north of Malta, not far from Mellieħa, the largest being at Mellieħa Bay itself.

Comino

For long periods of its history Comino was an unsafe place in which to live, nevertheless, people did inhabit this tiny island on and off, the population figures fluctuating from nil to sparse.

In 1416 the Maltese petitioned the Aragonese king, Alphonse V, to build a tower on Comino as a deterrent to the corsairs who made it their base, but the people of the Island has to wait two hundred years before work was taken in hand; eventually the Tower of Comino was finished under Grand Master Alof de Wignacourt in 1618.

Despite the protection of the tower, people were chary of making Comino their home, in fact, the ancient church here, was desecrated in 1667 as being derelict; in 1716 the church was repaired and reconsecrated and, by this time the island had been repopulated to some extent.

With its handful of resident families and a single hotel, Comino, even now, has an air of a forsaken but beautiful island.

Gozo

Some years ago it was planned to connect the islands of Malta and Gozo by a bridge and Japanese engineers were called in to carry out a feasibility study. The project was considered technically possible but as the expense involved would have been considerable the plan was shelved. And many people in Malta, and many more in Gozo breathed a sigh of relief.

Should the Island of Gozo become too accessible there is a real danger of the island losing the old-word charm which Gozo has so far retained, and which Malta possessed and, unfortunately, lost some half century ago. The sister island of Malta is different from the larger island in that it is more fertile, more picturesque, and far more unspoilt; but what makes Gozo so markedly different from Malta are the Gozitans.

Rustic, and living in the past, Gozo may be, but that does not make the Gozitans in any way backward: opera stars of international repute are invited to sing in the two theatres in Gozo's capital, Victoria (renamed from "Rabat" in honour of Queen Victoria). For the younger generation, pop singers and music festivals provide the more modern equivalent. Moreover, some of the best brains in Malta have come out of Gozo. Like rustic communities elsewhere, but especially where economic conditions are hard, Gozitans are thrifty, but their husbandry never encroaches on avarice, and their generosity towards worthy causes is always unstinted.

The citadel in Victoria is a museum in itself, it is here that the rich Medieval families of Gozo had their own quarters in which to spend the night. In the esplanade below, in the square known as it-Tokk, one can see the more colourful side of Gozo. In the open market and in the souvenir shops around it are exposed for sale such local handicrafts as crocheted woollen dresses, the wool spun from the local sheep and the dresses worked by the island's women, as is also the famous Gozo Lace, a traditional, but still a very much flourishing, art.

Even if the Malta-Gozo bridge has not been built, communication between the islands is easy and frequent as car-ferries, hover-craft and yachts crisscross the six kilometre wide Gozo Channel.

Xlendi (Facing page) - Is another summer resort used by the locals and tourists alike.

In 1961 two shipwrecks dating about 2nd century B.C. and 5th A.D. were located on the sea-bed at the mouth of Xlendi Creek under 35 metres of water. Many amphorae and several lead anchor stocks have been recovered from these wrecks and are now at the Gozo Museum of Archaeology.

Ta' Pinu Sanctuary

This is a national shrine and a centre of pilgrimages for both the Gozitans and the Maltese.
The present church was started in 1920 and consecrated in 1931. It was raised to the dignity of Basilica by Pope Pius IX a year later.

Qbajjar salt pans (Photo below) From a distance they look like small puddles when they are full with sea water.
The Qbajjar Salt Pans are the biggest salt-works in Gozo. Several tons of sea salt are produced there every year.

On the facing page, the beach of Ramla

Ġgantija Temples

The Ġgantija or, as it was commonly known in the past, "The Giants Tower", is the better preserved and by far the most impressive prehistoric temple. It is probably the finest of all ancient remains in these islands comparing with Stonehenge for grandeur. It was cleared round about 1826. Though no records survived of this operation, the most important find during this dig were the two stone heads of statuettes, now preserved at the Gozo Museum of Archaeology.

Għajn Tuffieħa

In Malta one cannot escape from history. When one goes for a swim, no matter where, one is always under the watchful eye of one of the coastal towers. These square two-storied towers are known as the "de Redin" towers because most of them (but **not** all) were built by Grand Master Martin de Redin during the middle of the 17th Century.

A cannon was fired by day and a beacon lit at night; and on the alarm being given, the towers to the left and to the right repeated the signal and within a short time the whole coastline was alerted in this way.

The Għajn Tuffieħa Tower overlooks two sandy beaches; one of the bays, the larger one, has had its name changed from it-Ramla Mixquqa (the Beach of Cracks, from the fissured cliffs surrounding it), to Military Bay when it was out of bounds as being in the Għajn Tuffieħa Camp (part of the old barracks have been converted into a holiday complex), and finally to the name it now bears: "Golden Bay".

(On the facing page.) The small port of Mgarr with the recently built harbour, has always been Gozo's only link with the outside world.

Rabat

The Rabat plateau is ideally suited for the building of a settlement, being, as it is, sited almost in the center of the island as well as being on high grounds that could be easily defended.

Man must have realized this soon after his arrival in Malta. Once it was inhabited the area has continued to be lived in ever since, generation after generation, and as one overlord replaced another.

Museum of Roman Antiquities. The misnamed Roman "villa" Museum covers the site of a rich and sumptuously decorated town house belonging to a wealthy person in Roman Malta.

The porticoed neo-classical façade was completed in 1925.

St. Paul's Collegiate Church

St Paul's Collegiate Church is constructed upon, but to the left of St Paul's Grotto, just outside the walls and in the ditch of the old city, hence its mention in old documents as St Paul outside the walls.

On the facing page: the crypt of St. Agatha's church; which is housed in the same convent and crypt where we can admire the beautiful frescoes which are twenty-nine in all, go back to 1480 A.D. and are attribuited in majority to Salvatore d'Antonio.

Mdina

On the top: the Main Gate to the City was erected in 1724 by Grand Master de Vilhena, replacing an earlier draw-bridge gate the outline of which, now walled up, is still visible some metres away to the right of the present gate.

Cathedral Church

According to tradition Malta's earliest Cathedral (facing page) was dedicated to the Blessed Virgin, Mother of God, dilapidated in the Muslim period and reconstructed and rededicated to St Paul after the Norman conquest.

The Cathedral Museum in Archbishop Square is an imposing baroque palace housing rich collections of art and archaeology as well as important archives. (Below on the facing, page).

Some characteristic aspects
of the town of Mdina.

Falzon Palace
(Norman House)

An attraction of Mdina are the many and various, older and more recents brass knockers affixed to the city's palaces and houses.

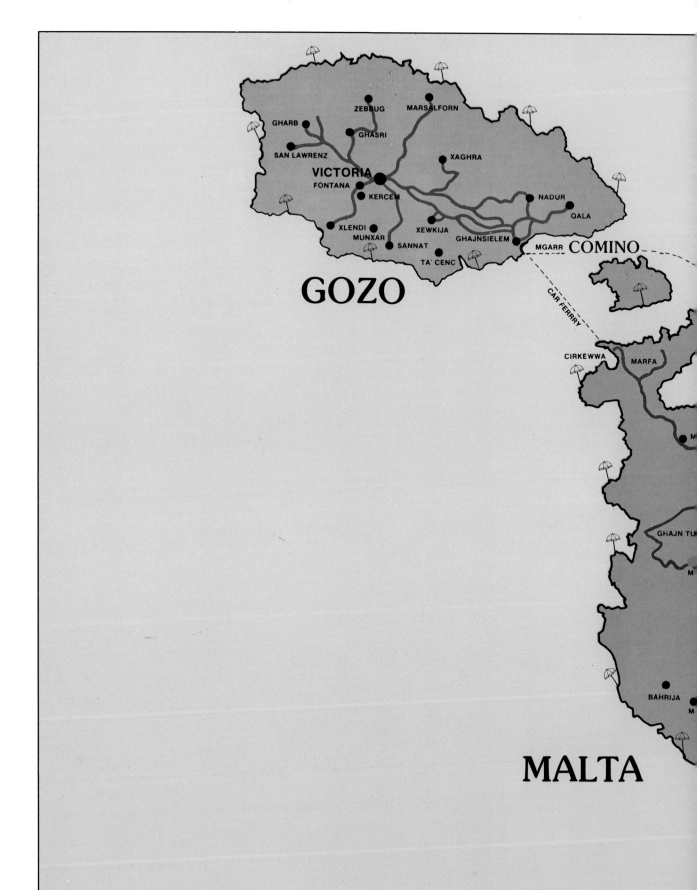

ZEBBUG
MARSALFORN
GHARB
GHASRI
SAN LAWRENZ
XAGHRA
VICTORIA
FONTANA
KERCEM
NADUR
QALA
XLENDI
MUNXAR
XEWKIJA
SANNAT
GHAJNSIELEM
TA' CENC
MGARR

COMINO

GOZO

CIRKEWWA
MARFA

GHAJN TU

BAHRIJA

MALTA

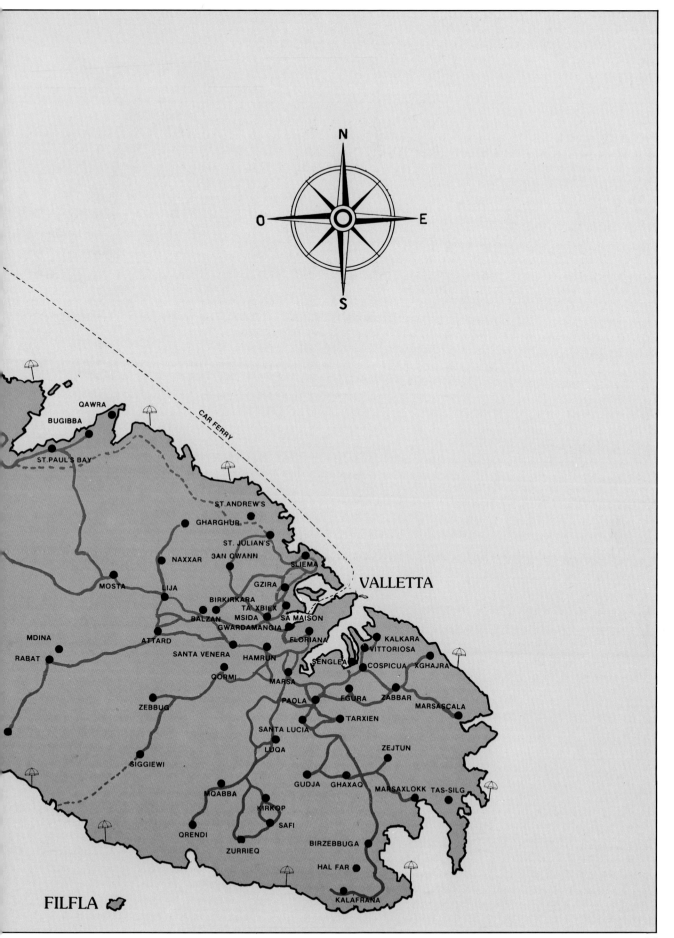

N

O   E

S

QAWRA
BUGIBBA
ST.PAUL'S BAY
CAR FERRY
ST.ANDREW'S
GHARGHUR
ST. JULIAN'S
NAXXAR
3AN QWANN
SLIEMA
GZIRA
VALLETTA
MOSTA
LIJA
BIRKIRKARA
TA'XBIEX
BALZAN
MSIDA
SA MAISON
GWARDAMANGIA
MDINA
ATTARD
FLORIANA
KALKARA
RABAT
SANTA VENERA
HAMRUN
VITTORIOSA
SENGLEA
QORMI
COSPICUA
XGHAJRA
MARSA
PAOLA
FGURA
ZABBAR
MARSASCALA
ZEBBUG
TARXIEN
SANTA LUCIA
LUQA
ZEJTUN
SIGGIEWI
GUDJA
GHAXAQ
MARSAXLOKK
TAS-SILG
MQABBA
KIRKOP
SAFI
QRENDI
BIRZEBBUGA
ZURRIEQ
HAL FAR
FILFLA
KALAFRANA

INDEX

VALLETTA 10

MARSAXLOKK 31

TA' QALI 39

SLIEMA AND S. JULIAN 18

WIED IZ-ZURRIEQ 34

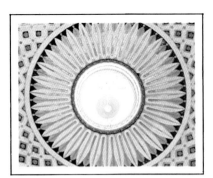

MOSTA 41

THE THREE CITIES 23

ĦAĠAR QIM 37

BUĠIBBA 43

TARXIEN 26

MNAJDRA 38

ST. PAUL'S BAY 44

MELLIEHA 45

GHAJN TUFFIEHA 53

COMINO 46

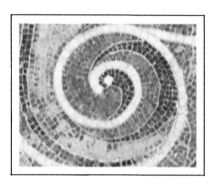

RABAT 54

GOZO 48

MDINA 56

GĠANTIJA 51

Photographs by Bruna Polimeni.

Our thanks to
Miller Distributors Limited
for kind permission
to use the following photographs:
pages 11-18-20 bottom; 21-22-34
top; 43 top; 49 top; 50 top; 64.